SOLO SPEECHES FOR WOMEN
1800-1914

SOLO SPEECHES FOR WOMEN
1800-1914

Edited by Shaun McKenna

OBERON BOOKS
LONDON

First published in 1997 in association with the London Academy of
Music and Dramatic Art, by Oberon Books Ltd.
(incorporating Absolute Classics),
521 Caledonian Road, London N7 9RH
Tel: 0171 607 3637/Fax: 0171 607 3629

e-mail: oberon.books@btinternet.com

Reprinted with corrections, 1999

A catalogue record for this book is available from the British Library

ISBN 1 84002 003 2

Cover design: Andrzej Klimowski

Typography: Richard Doust

Printed in Great Britain by MPG Ltd., Bodmin

INTRODUCTION

This collection of solo acting pieces from the nineteenth century is designed to provide actors, teachers and examination candidates with effective and less well-known material. For candidates approaching LAMDA examinations, the earlier speeches will be found useful and approachable by candidates from Grade 6 onwards. The scenes increase in emotional complexity and technical challenges as the collection progresses, and later scenes will be found appropriate for Medal examinations and Diplomas, and as audition speeches.

Until the latter part of the century, when the great revolutionary playwrights – Ibsen, Strindberg, Chekhov, Wilde and Shaw – came to the fore, nineteenth-century theatre was dominated more by star performers than by remarkable playwrights. This is particularly true of the English repertoire. As a result, this collection contains a substantial number of speeches from European plays. Where such names as Chekhov, Strindberg and Wilde appear, I have selected speeches from minor or little-known plays, rather than the *Miss Julies* and *Doll's Houses* which are universally popular sources of solo scenes.

The language of much nineteenth-century drama seems melodramatic and stilted to contemporary ears, making it difficult to play. The speeches in this collection have been selected to minimise this. Many of the English speeches are from comedies, where writers seem less entrenched in 'elevated' modes of expression. The European speeches have been specially translated for this collection by Simon Parker, Mary Patrick and Veronica George. References to sources and complete editions of plays are included.

The dearth of female playwrights in this period is noticeable. It is also evident that male playwrights tend to portray women as virginal victims, flirtatious young minxes, broadly-drawn 'older characters' or 'women with a past'.

Many of these characters appear to be concerned only with finding, securing or despising a husband. One looks, more often than not, outside the English repertoire for sympathetic portrayals of women of intelligence and integrity.

Shaun McKenna

CONTENTS

8   SHAUN McKENNA

THE AREA BELLE (1864)

by William Brough and Andrew Halliday

William Brough (1826-1870) and Andrew Halliday (1830-1877) wrote thirteen one-act farces between 1861 and 1865, eight of them performed at the Adelphi Theatre. Brough wrote a further sixty plays, burlesques and extravaganzas while Halliday was subsequently best known for the 1867 drama, *The Great City*. The Brough-Halliday farces deal with servants, tradesmen and cockneys. The plays are cheerful, slight and almost entirely forgotten. *The Area Belle* was enormously popular on its first appearance, playing 128 times in the 1864 season.

Penelope is a pretty young maid, much admired by tradesmen and locally known as the Area Belle. This speech opens the play, where she is discovered cleaning dish covers and singing.

PENELOPE (*Singing*): 'I'd choose to be a daisy, if I might be a flower.' If I might be a flower, indeed! Why, everybody says I *am* a flower! Pitcher says I'm like the rose. Tosser calls me his tulip. Chalks says my breath's like buttercups, while the baker's young man came in the other day while I was making pies, and said I was flour all over. Oh, it's very nice to be so universally admired; not, perhaps, that it's much to be wondered at. And yet it's rather puzzling to have so many sweethearts! One doesn't know how to choose amongst 'em; and I'm obliged to keep a book, what fine folks call a dairy, for fear I should forget whose turn it is to come and visit me. Let me see – there's Pitcher in the police, and Tosser in the Grenadiers, and there's Dobbs the baker, and Chumps the butcher – they all come by turns. And there's the milkman: he, I believe, is rather sweet upon me, but I have never put the milkman in the dairy yet.

(*Looks at book.*) Now then, whose turn is it tonight? Missus is going out, and I shall have a nice long evening. (*Reads.*) 'Pitcher'. Ah, he is a nice young man! I do think, if I have a preference, it's Pitcher. (*Looks at book, and starts.*) What's this? Good gracious, if I haven't asked Tosser too! Now, if there is another man in the world besides Pitcher that I adore, it's Tosser! What am I to do? If Pitcher or Tosser meet tonight there will be bloodshed. I must forego the happiness of receiving either, and have recourse to the pepper box. (*Puts pepper box on window sill.*) There, that's our signal – that's the red light on our railway, and means 'danger'. Whosever's turn it is to come, that signal in the window informs him that Missus or some other heavy luggage train is in the way, and he shunts off accordingly.

A knocking at the door.

There's the milkman, but he only comes professionally. He's not upon my private visiting list yet.

Available in *English Plays of the Nineteenth Century, Volume 4.* Edited by M. R. Booth (Oxford University Press).

THE TICKET OF LEAVE MAN (1863)

by Tom Taylor

Tom Taylor (1817-1880) was born in Sunderland and called to the Bar in 1846. He was a prolific and successful dramatist and sometime actor. His plays include *Sir Roger de Coverley* (1851), *Helping Hands* (1855), *Going to the Bad* (1858) and *Handsome is that Handsome Does* (1870). *The Ticket of Leave Man* is his most famous play, adapted from a French original and still occasionally revived. It combines melodrama, sentiment, social observation and humour.

> *BOB BRIERLY, a young Lancashire man, has become embroiled with criminals while trying to forge a life in London. He has been sent to prison for three years, and is sustained by the fond friendship of MAY EDWARDS, a respectable young street-singer and seamstress. Here, in her lodgings, MAY reads one of BOB's letters. She is discovered with a birdcage on the table, arranging a piece of sugar and groundsel between the bars.*

MAY (*To the bird*): There, Goldie, I must give *you* your breakfast, though I don't care a bit for my own. Ah! you find singing a better trade than I did, you little rogue. I'm sure I shall have a letter from Robert this morning. I've all his letters here. (*Takes out a packet from her work-box.*) How he has improved in his handwriting since the first. (*Opening letter.*) That's more than three years back. Oh, what an old woman I'm getting! It's no use denying it, Goldie. If you'll be quiet, like a good, well-bred canary, I'll read you Robert's last letter. 'Portland, February 25th, 1860. My own dearest May, (*Kissing it.*) As the last year keeps slipping away, I think more and more of our happy meeting; but for your love and comfort I think I should have broken down.' There, Goldie, do you hear that? (*She kisses the letter.*) 'But now we both see how things are

guided for the best. But for my being sent to
prison, I should have died before this, a broken-
down drunkard, if not worse; and you might still
have been earning hard bread as a street-singer,
or carried from a hospital ward to a pauper's
grave.' Yes, yes, (*Shuddering.*) that's true. 'This
place has made a man of me, and you have found
friends and the means of earning a livelihood. I
count the days till we meet. Good-bye and
heaven bless you, prays your ever affectionate
Robert Brierly.' (*Kisses the letter frequently.*) And
don't I count the days too? There! (*Makes a mark
in her pocket almanack.*) Another gone! They seem
so slow – when one looks forward – and yet they
pass so quickly! (*Taking up birdcage.*) Come,
Goldie, while I work you must sing me a nice
song for letting you hear that nice letter.

Available in *English Plays of the Nineteenth Century, Volume 2.*
Edited by M. R. Booth (Oxford University Press).

THE TICKET OF LEAVE MAN (1863)

by Tom Taylor

See notes on Tom Taylor and *The Ticket of Leave Man* on page 11.

EMILY ST EVREMOND is a boisterous but somewhat faded music hall artiste, fallen on hard times. She is a neighbour of the heroine, MAY EDWARDS, in MRS WILLOUGHBY's rooming house.

EMILY: May I come in? Call me Mrs St Evremond, please, Miss Edwards, Jones has changed his name. When people have come down in circumstances, the best way that can do is to keep up their names. Like St Evremond, it looks well in the bill, and sounds foreign. That's always attractive – and I dress my hair à la Française, to keep up the effect. I've brought back the shawl you were kind enough to lend me.

I didn't get the engagement. The proprietor said my appearance was quite the thing – good stage face and figure, and all that: you know how those creatures always flatter one; but they hadn't an opening just now in the comic duet and character dance business.

Disappointed? My husband? Oh! bless you, he doesn't know what I've been after. I couldn't bear to worrit him, poor fellow! He's had so many troubles. *I've* been used to rough it – before we came into our fortune.

Noise heard overhead.

Don't be alarmed – it's only Green; I left him to practise the clog-dance while I went out. He's so clumsy. He often comes down like that in the double shuffles. But he gets on very nicely in the comic duets. He's willing enough to turn his hand

to anything, only he is so slow in turning his legs.
Ah, my dear, you're very lucky only having
yourself to keep. And you that was brought up to a
public life too. Every night about six, when they
begin to light up the gas, I feel so fidgety, you
can't think – I want to be off to the theatre. I
couldn't live away from the float, that is, not if I
had to work for my living – of course it was very
different the three years we had our fortune. We
were both fast, dear; and to do Jones justice, I don't
think he was the fastest. You see he was used to
spending and I wasn't. It seemed so jolly at first to
have everything one liked.

Available in *English Plays of the Nineteenth Century, Volume 2*.
Edited by M. R. Booth (Oxford University Press).

THE CABINET MINISTER (1890)

by Sir Arthur Wing Pinero

Sir Arthur Wing Pinero (1854-1934) was born in Islington and was of Portuguese extraction. After completing his studies, he worked with his father in a lawyer's office but in 1874 joined the acting company of the Theatre Royal, Edinburgh. He acted with many of the great names of Victorian theatre, including Sir Henry Irving and Squire Bancroft. After 1882 he concentrated on writing and was knighted in 1909. His famous plays include *Trelawney of the Wells* (1898), *Dandy Dick* (1887), *The Magistrate* (1885), *The Schoolmistress* (1886) and *The Enchanted Cottage*.

> The Cabinet Minister *is a farce about corruption in politics – a dangerous treatment of such a subject for its period. IMOGEN is the daughter of SIR JULIAN TWOMBLEY, Secretary of State for an un-named department. Here she writes to her beloved, VALENTINE WHITE, from whom she has been separated by circumstances. The scene is the inner hall at Drumdurris Castle, Perthshire. IMOGEN is sitting at a table reading over a letter she has written.*

IMOGEN: 'Dear Mr White.' I shall never call him Valentine again, except in my thoughts. (*Reading.*) 'Dear Mr White, I am sorry to hear that you are discontented with your recent appointment to the Deputy-Assistant-Head-Gamekeepership on the Drumdurris estate, and that you consider it a sinecure fit only for a debilitated peer.' Now for it. (*Resuming.*) 'Permit me to take this opportunity of informing you that I have at length consented to an engagement between myself and Sir Colin Macphail of Ballocheevin.' Oh, how awful it looks in ink! (*Resuming.*) 'As it is becoming that I should support such a position with dignity I would prefer not encountering your dislike to "stuck-up people" by ever seeing you again.' Oh, Val. 'I therefore suggest that you obtain a nastier appointment than that of Deputy-Assistant-Head-Gamekeeper at Drumdurris without delay.' That will do – beautifully. (*In tears.*) Oh, Val, why have you never spoken? I know you are poor, but I would have gone away with you and lived cheerfully and economically in that rock if you had but asked me. Why, why have you never asked me?

She sits on a footstool looking into the fire.

After all, as he has never been a lover, why shouldn't I see him and mention my engagement in a calm, cool, ladylike way? (*Tearing up the letter passionately.*) I must see him once more – in a calm, cool, ladylike way. I'll write just a line asking him to come to me this morning.

The Cabinet Minister is published by Oberon Books.

THE TICKET OF LEAVE MAN (1863)

by Tom Taylor

See notes on Tom Taylor and *The Ticket of Leave Man* on page 11.

MRS WILLOUGHBY, a splendidly garrulous comic grotesque, runs a respectable rooming-house, in which the play's heroine, MAY EDWARDS, resides. She is talking about her grandson, SAM WILLOUGHBY.

MRS WILLOUGHBY: Sam, ah, that boy – I came here about him; hasn't he been here this morning? Ah, Miss Edwards, if you would only talk to him; he don't mind anything I say, no more than if it was a flat-iron, which what that boy have cost me in distress of mind, and clothes, and caps, and breakages, never can be known – and his poor mother which was the only one I brought up and had five, she says to me, 'Mother,' she says, 'he's a big child,' she says, 'and he's a beautiful child, but he have a temper of his own'; which 'Mary,' I says – she was called Mary, like you, my dear, after her aunt, from which we had expectations, but which was left to the Blind Asylum, and the Fishmongers' Alms Houses, and very like you she was, only she had light hair and blue eyes – 'Mary, my dear,' I says, 'I hope you'll never live to see it', and took she was at twenty-three, sudden, and that boy I've had to mend and wash and do for ever since, and hard lines it is. You may suppose he has an excellent heart – which I wish it had been his heart I found in his right-'and pocket as I was a-mending his best trousers last night, which it was a short-pipe, which it is nothing but the truth, and smoked to that degree as if it had been black-leaded, which many's the time when he've come in, I've said, 'Sam,' I've said, 'I smell tobacco', I've said. 'Grandmother,' he'd say to me, quite grave and innocent, 'P'raps it's the chimbley' – and him a child of fifteen, and a short pipe in his right-'and pocket! I'm sure I could have broke my heart over it, I could; let alone the pipe – which I flung it into the fire – but a happy moment since is a thing I have not known. And how you can trust him to carry parcels; but, Oh, Miss Edwards, if you'd talk to him, and tell him short pipes is the thief of time, and tobacco's the root of all evil.

Available in *English Plays of the Nineteenth Century, Volume 2*. Edited by M. R. Booth (Oxford University Press).

THE CASSILIS ENGAGEMENT (1907)

by St John Hankin

St John Emile Clavering Hankin (1869-1909) was born in Southampton and educated at Malvern and Merton College, Oxford. He was a journalist and commercial playwright, whose performed works include such little-remembered plays as *The Return of the Prodigal* (1905), *The Last of the De Mullins* (1908) and *The Charity that Began at Home* (1906). His comedies were enormously popular in their day and his characters have life and sparkle, even if the plots now seem thin.

The play is set in Deynham Abbey, home of the Cassilis family. A great deal of upset has been caused by the engagement of young GEOFFREY CASSILIS to ETHEL BORRIDGE, a young London girl and his social inferior. However, this being a comedy of social misunderstandings, all is resolved in the last act when the forthright ETHEL makes her feelings clear to GEOFFREY.

ETHEL (*Turning on him impatiently*): My dear Geoff, is it impossible for you to understand that I don't *want* to marry you? That if I married you I should be bored to death? That I loathe the life down here among your highly respectable friends? That if I had to live here with you I should yawn myself into my grave in six months? Oh, it's pretty enough, I suppose, and the fields are very green, and the view from Milverton Hill is much admired. And you live all alone in a great park, and you've horses and dogs, and a butler and two footmen. But that's not enough for me. I want life, people, lots of people. If I lived down here I should go blue-mouldy in three weeks. I'm town-bred, a true Cockney. I want streets and shops and gas lamps. I don't want your carriage and pair. Give me a penny omnibus. Now you're shocked. It *is* vulgar, isn't it? But *I'm* vulgar. And I'm not ashamed of it. Now you know. All over and

done with. I surrender my claim to everything, the
half of your wordly goods, of your mother's wordly
goods, of your house, your park, your men-servants
and maid-servants, your aristocratic relations. Don't
let's forget your aristocratic relations. I surrender
them all. There's my hand on it.

(*With genuine surprise.*) My dear Geoff, you don't
mean to say you're *sorry*! You ought to be flinging
your cap in the air at regaining your liberty. Why,
I believe there are tears in your eyes! Actually
tears! Let me look. (*Suddenly serious.*) Geoff, do you
want to marry me still? Do you *love* me still? No,
Geoff. Think before you speak.

There, you see! Come, dear, cheer up. It's best as it
is. Give me a kiss. The last one. And now I'll run
upstairs and tell mother. (*Laughs.*) Poor mother!
Won't she make a shine.

Available in *Late Victorian Plays 1890-1914*. Edited by George
Rowell (Oxford University Press).

HOW TO SETTLE ACCOUNTS WITH YOUR LAUNDRESS (1847)

by Joseph Stirling Coyne

Joseph Stirling Coyne (1803-1868) was a successful journalist and dramatist and wrote a number of one-act farces, of which *How to Settle Accounts...* is the best. Between 1835 and 1869 he turned out around thirty-five farces (many of them performed at the Adelphi Theatre) as well as a similar number of burlesques, extravaganzas and melodramas. *How To Settle Accounts...* was popular in London and subsequently in France and Germany.

> *The scene is a tailor's showroom in London's fashionable Jermyn Street. WHITTINGTON WIDGETTS, a West End tailor, is preparing for an assignation with the flirtatious MLLE CHERIE BOUNCE. However, his laundress, MARY WHITE, calls at an inconvenient time. MARY, who has known WIDGETTS since less prosperous days, is a pleasant girl – but nobody's fool!*

MARY: Now, Widgy dear – oh, good gracious, what a love of a waistcoat you've on! Let me look at it, do! Well, it's a real beauty. You used not to wear such waistcoats as that when you lived in Fuller's Rents.

Do you know, Widgy, I don't think you're at all improved since you fell in for that fortune by a legacy you never expected. When you lived in Fuller's Rents you used to walk out with me on a Sunday; you never walk with me at all now. And you sometimes used to take me at half-price to the theatres. And you remember how we used to go together to Greenwich, with a paper of ham sandwiches in my basket, and sit under the trees in the park, and talk, and laugh – law, how we used to laugh, to be sure – and then you used to talk of love and constancy and connubial felicity in a little back parlour, and a heap of beautiful things. And you know, Widgy dear, when we enter that happy state – I allude to the marriage state, of course. You don't forget, I hope, that I have your promissory note on the back of twenty-nine unpaid washing bills to make me your lawful wife. (*Produces several papers.*) There they are – and there's the last of them. 'Six months after date I promise to marry Miss Mary White.' There, sir, you're due next Monday. I can't be put off any longer, and understand me, Mr Widgetts, I won't neither.

Well, now that matter's settled, I'll go and collect your soiled things, for it's getting late.

WIDGETTS exits.

(*Collecting his clothes.*) Well, you're a pretty careless fellow, to leave your letters in your waistcoat pocket. Where is he gone to? (*Examines the note curiously.*) 'Whittington Widgetts, Esq.' It's a woman's hand. I've a good mind to read it. I've no secrets from him and he has none from me – or at least he oughtn't to; so it can be no harm. (*Opens note and reads hastily.*) 'Ma'amselle Cherie Bounce' – ah! – 'compliments happy to sup with Mr W. W. this evening – female notions – single gent – lobsters is stronger than prudence – therefore trusts to indulgence, at nine o'clock precise.' Oh, the minx! 'PS I'll come in my blue *visite* and my native innocence.' Oh, Widgetts, the false deceitful wretch! To deceive me and wash out all his promises; to wring my heart and mangle my affections like that. (*Sobbing.*) But I – I – don't care not a pin's point, no – I despise him and hate him worse than poison, and I'll – I'll – I'll – tell him so.

Available in *English Plays of the Nineteenth Century, Volume 4*. Edited by M. R. Booth (Oxford University Press).

HINDLE WAKES (1912)

by Stanley Houghton

Stanley Houghton (1881-1913) was born in Cheshire and worked in his father's cotton business before becoming involved in the growing repertory theatre movement of the early 1900s. His plays include *The Reckoning* (1906), *Fancy Free* (1911) and *The Fifth Commandment* (1913). *Hindle Wakes* is his best play, still frequently performed. It is the best-known representative of the so-called 'Manchester School' of dramatists and, for its era, dealt with contentious and controversial material.

Hindle Wakes is a study of two families in the north country town of Hindle – the mill-owning Jeffcotes and the working class Hawthorns. FANNY HAWTHORN, a girl in her 20s, is discovered to have spent a weekend away with ALAN JEFFCOTE. When scandal threatens, the families try to patch together a match – a match that suits nobody but which appears to be required by social convention. However, the forthright FANNY astonishes everyone with this outburst in the final act. This piece requires a Lancashire dialect.

FANNY: Don't you kid yourself, my lad! It isn't because I'm afraid of spoiling your life that I'm refusing you, but because I'm afraid of spoiling *mine*! That didn't occur to you?

Suppose it didn't last? Weddings brought about this road have a knack of turning out badly. Would you ever forget it was your father bade you marry me? No fear! You'd bear me a grudge all my life for that. You wouldn't be able to help it. It mostly happens that road. Look at old Mrs Eastwood – hers was a case like ours. Old Joe Eastwood's father made them wed. And she's been separated from him these thirty years, living all alone in that big house at Valley Edge. Got any amount of brass, she has, but she's so lonesome-like she does her own housework for the sake of something to occupy her time. The tradesfolk catch her washing the front steps. You don't find me making a mess of my life like that. I can manage all right on twenty-five bob a week.

Love you? Good heavens, of course not! Why on earth should I love you? You were just someone to have a bit of fun with. You were an amusement – a lark. How much more did you care for me? You're a man, and I was your little fancy. Well, I'm a woman, and you were my little fancy. You wouldn't prevent a woman enjoying herself as well as a man, if she takes it into her head? Are you shocked?

You're not good enough for me. The chap Fanny Hawthorn weds has got to be made of different stuff from you, my lad. My husband, if ever I have one, will be a man, not a fellow who'll throw over his girl at his father's bidding! Strikes me the sons of these rich manufacturers are all much alike. They seem a bit weak in the upper storey. It's their fathers' brass that's too much for them, happen! They don't know how to spend it properly. They're like chaps who can't carry their drink because they aren't used to it. The brass gets into their heads, like!

You're not a fool altogether. But there's summat lacking. You're not man enough for me. You're a nice lad, and I'm fond of you. But I couldn't ever marry you. We've had a right good time together, I'll never forget that. It has been a right good time, and no mistake! We've enjoyed ourselves proper! But all good times have to come to an end, and ours is over now. Come along now, and bid me farewell. (*Holding out her hand.*) Goodbye, old lad.

Available in *Late Victorian Plays 1890-1914*. Edited by George Rowell (Oxford University Press).

MR PAUL PRY (1826)

by Douglas William Jerrold

Douglas William Jerrold (1803-1857) was house dramatist at the Coburg Theatre where *Mr Paul Pry* was first performed. He was very badly paid and even his major success, *Black Eyed Susan,* brought in only twenty pounds. He later gave up writing plays in favour of journalism.

> Mr Paul Pry *was a farcical version of a comedy by John Poole, which was first performed at the Haymarket Theatre in 1825. The eponymous hero is a meddlesome nuisance. CRIMP is maid to LAURA, the beautiful ward of the 'very odd' MR OLDBUTTON, and involves herself in her charge's romantic aspirations.*

CRIMP: I saw Captain Haselton at the window as we drove up, and he looked almost as amiable as he used to appear when he paid me for planning assignations and back-staircase escapes. But you say Mr Oldbutton has destined you for Sir Spangle Rainbow? Now, if he were the last man in the world I wouldn't have him! No, I – eh! The last man, did I say – why, perhaps that's promising too much. But lord, madam, talking about being designed for Sir Spangle – I've no notion of such designing indeed. It's having a wife per order – it's likening us dear little women to so many parcels of grocery in thus packing us up, labelling, and sending us home to one particular customer. Do you take my advice, madam – run away with Captain Haselton, and get married at once. Why, the idea is shocking to be sure, but I've heard say that marriage is like bathing in cold water; we stand shivering a long time at the edge, when it's only one plunge, and all is over. I know that Mr Oldbutton, as uncle to Captain Haselton, is highly incensed with him for having gambled away his fortune. But no matter; as I know you wish to see the Captain, I will endeavour to decoy him hither. Leave it to me. Do you retire within your chamber, and I'll go and reconnoitre. Oh, how fortunate you ought to think yourself in having so prudent and clever a person as myself! Now don't stir till I come back.

Exit LAURA.

A young lady in love is as profitable to her chambermaid as a consumptive patient to the physician. All we have to do is to take the fees and let the malady work its own cure.

Available in *English Plays of the Nineteenth Century, Volume 4.* Edited by M. R. Booth (Oxford University Press).

ENGAGED (1877)

by Sir W. S. Gilbert

Sir William Schwenk Gilbert (1836-1911) is best known for his collaboration with Sir Arthur Sullivan on The Savoy Operas. However, he was a distinguished humorist and playwright in his own right, and has been frequently revived this century. His solo works include *Tom Cobb* (1875), *Randall's Thumb* (1871) and *The Blue-Legged Lady* (1874).

> *MISS TREHERNE elopes to Gretna Green with BELVAWNEY but is wooed by his friend, CHEVIOT HILL. HILL explains to MISS TREHERNE that BELVAWNEY, on his marriage, will lose his income. The income will then go to the Symperson family. HILL is engaged to the Symperson daughter, MINNIE. Arriving at the Symperson's house, MISS TREHERNE explains her predicament to MINNIE, unaware that she is talking about MINNIE's betrothed. MISS TREHERNE is a self-dramatising creature.*

MISS TREHERNE: At last I'm in my darling's home, the home of the bright blythe carolling thing that lit, as with a ray of heaven's sunlight, the murky gloom of my miserable schooldays. But what do I see? Tarts? Ginger wine? There are rejoicings of some kind afoot. Alas, I am out of place here. What have I in common with tarts? Oh, I am ill-attuned to scenes of revelry! (*Takes a tart and eats it.*)

MINNIE enters.

Minnie! My own long-lost lamb! This is the first gleam of joy that has lighted my darksome course this many and many a day! And in spite of the change that time and misery have brought upon me, you knew me at once! (*Eating the tart all this time.*)

How wondrously fair you have grown! And this dress! Why, it is surely a bridal dress! Those tarts – that wine! Surely this is not your wedding day?

Oh, strange chance! Oh, unheard-of coincidence!
Married! And to whom? Happy – strangely happy
girl! You, at least, know your husband's name. It is
much to know. I do not know mine. Forgotten it?
No; I never knew it. It is a dark mystery. It may
not be fathomed. It is buried in the fathomless gulf
of the Eternal Past. There let it lie.

It is a lurid tale. Three months since I fled from a
hated one who was to have married me. He
pursued me. I confided my distress to a young and
wealthy stranger. Acting on his advice, I declared
myself to be his wife; he declared himself to be my
husband. We were parted immediately afterwards,
and we have never met since. But this took place in
Scotland, and by the law of that remarkable
country we are man and wife, though I didn't know
it at the time.

Fun? Say, rather, horror – distraction – chaos! I am
rent with conflicting doubts! Perhaps he was
already married; in that case I am a bigamist.
Maybe he is dead; in that case I am a widow.
Maybe he is alive; in that case I am a wife. What
am I? Am I single? Am I married? Am I a widow?
Can I marry? Have I married? May I marry? Who
am I? Where am I? What am I? What is my name?
What is my condition in life? If I am married, to
whom am I married? If I am a widow, how came I
to be a widow, and whose widow came I to be?
Why am I his widow? What did he die of? Did he
leave me anything? If anything, how much, and is
it saddled with conditions? Can I marry again
without forfeiting it? Have I a mother-in-law?
Have I a family of step-children, and if so, how
many, and what are their ages, sexes, sizes, names
and dispositions? These are questions that rack me
night and day, and until they are settled, peace and
I are not on terms!

But enough of my selfish sorrows. (*Goes up to table and takes a tart.*) Tell me about the noble boy who is about to make you his. Has he any dross?

Available in *English Plays of the Nineteenth Century, Volume 3*. Edited by M. R. Booth (Oxford University Press).

HERNANI (1830)

by Victor Hugo

Victor Hugo (1802-1885), the famous French novelist and playwright, is best known for his epic novels *Les Miserables* (1862) and *Notre Dame de Paris* (1831). He was a prolific playwright, with works including *Le Roi s'Amuse* (1832) which formed the basis of Verdi's opera, *Rigoletto*, and *Ruy Blas* (1860). *Hernani* was also the basis of a Verdi opera. Hugo was a controversial, radical figure and suffered greatly at the hands of the censor.

> *DOÑA SOL is beloved by three men – HERNANI, a bandit leader (whose love she returns); her elderly guardian, RUY GOMEZ, to whom she is betrothed; and the King of Spain, DON CARLOS. Here she passionately refuses the hand of DON CARLOS.*

DOÑA SOL:

'Twixt us, Don Carlos, there can nothing be.
For you, my father freely shed his blood.
I am of noble birth and will defend
The honour of my name. I am too high
To be your concubine but yet too low
To be your wife. Sir, you had best approach
Some worthless girl to join in your debauch.
For if you dare insult me, you will learn
What honour means to someone of my ilk.
What, be your queen? No, no, it is a snare.
Let me speak frankly. I would rather go
Into the mountains with my King, Hernani,
And wander like an outcast of the law,
Starve with him, suffer with him, beg my bread,
Sharing each hardship of his destiny,
War, exile, terror, endless days of sorrow,
Than be an Empress to an Emperor.
I do not love you, sir. Oh, pity me!

You're King, and all you have to do is choose
Between the duchesses and countesses,
The great Court ladies who will match your love
And feel great honour in returning it.
The man I love and am forbidden has
No such advantages. Sir, you possess
Castile and Aragon, Murcia and Léon,
Navarre and Flanders – ten more kingdoms, yes,
And India with all its gold and jewels.
A matchless empire, and so wide and vast
The sun, I swear, can never set on it.
You have all this, and yet you would take me
From one who, but for me, has nothing.

Throwing herself on her knees.

From you, to guard the honour I so prize,
I'll nothing take except this jewelled dirk.

She snatches the dagger from his belt.

Approach me and I kill you – and myself.
Hernani! Oh, Hernani!

Another translation of this play is available in *World Drama*.
Edited by Barrett H. Clark (Dover Books).

THE MAGISTRATE (1885)

by Sir Arthur Wing Pinero

See note on Pinero on page 15.

*AGATHA, now 36, is married to the magistrate of the title,
ÆNEAS POSKET. Here she explains to her sister,
CHARLOTTE, the fix in which she finds herself.*

AGATHA: Well, Charley, you know I lost my poor
dear first husband at a very delicate age. Yes, that's
what I mean. Five-and-thirty is a very delicate age
to find yourself single. You're neither one thing nor
the other. You're not exactly a two-year-old, and
you don't care to pull a hansom. However, I soon
met Mr Posket at Spa – bless him! Yes, Charley,
and in less than a month I went triumphantly over
the course. But, Charley dear, I didn't carry the
fair weight for age – and that's my trouble.
Undervaluing Æneas' love, in a moment of, I hope,
not unjustifiable vanity, I took five years from my
total, which made me thirty-one on my wedding
morning.

Yes, Charley, but don't you see the consequences? It
has thrown everything out. As I am now thirty-one,
instead of thirty-six as I ought to be, it stands to
reason that I couldn't have been married twenty
years ago, which I was. So I have had to fib in
proportion. If I am only thirty-one now, my boy
couldn't have been born nineteen years ago, and if
he could, he oughtn't to have been, because on my
own showing I wasn't married till four years later.
Now you see the result! Isn't it awkward! And his
moustache is becoming more and more obvious
every day.

He believes his mother, of course, as a boy should.
As a prudent woman, I always kept him in

ignorance of his age in case of necessity. But it is terribly hard on the poor child, because his aims, instincts, and ambitions are all so horribly in advance of his condition. His food, his books, his amusements are out of keeping with his palate, his brain, and his disposition; and with all this suffering – his wretched mother has the remorseful consciousness of having shortened her offspring's life. Because, if he lives to be a hundred, he must be buried at ninety-five.

Then there's another aspect. He's a great favourite with all our friends – women friends especially. Even his little music mistress and the girl-servants hug and kiss him because he's such an engaging boy, and I can't stop it. But it's very awful to see these innocent women fondling a young man of nineteen. The other day I found my poor boy sitting on Lady Jenkins's lap, and in the presence of Sir George. I have no right to compromise Lady Jenkins in that way. And now, Charley, you see the whirlpool in which I am struggling – if you can throw me a rope, pray do.

Available in *English Plays of the Nineteenth Century, Volume 4.* Edited by M. R. Booth (Oxford University Press).

TOM COBB (1875)

by Sir W S Gilbert

See note on Gilbert on page 27.

At the house of COLONEL O'FIP, an Irish adventurer, penniless young surgeon TOM COBB is in love with O'FIP's daughter, MATILDA. CAROLINE is described as 'a romantic-looking young lady, with long curls and gushing, poetical demeanour.' This is her first arrival in the household. She pauses melodramatically.

CAROLINE: Matilda! Don't ye know me?

I came to town yesterday; and though ten long weary years have flown since last we met, I could not pass my dear old friend's abode without one effort to awake those slumbering chords that, struck in unison, ever found ready echoes in our sister hearts. How well – how very well you're looking – and heavens, how lovely!

Am I married? Alas, no. Oh, Matilda, a maiden's heart should be as free as the summer sun itself; and it's sad when, in youth's heyday, its trilling gladness has been trodden underfoot by the iron shod heel of a serpent. Swear that, come what may, no torture shall ever induce you to reveal the secret I am going to confide to you.

Will you believe me when I tell you that – I have loved? And that I have been loved in return? He was a poet-soldier, fighting the Paynim foe in India's burning clime – a glorious songster, who swept the lute with one hand while he sabred the foe with the other!

In the band, Matilda? He was a major-general! Handsome? I know not. I never saw him. I never saw his face; but – I have seen his soul! It is like the frenzied passion of the antelope! Like the wild

fire of the tiger-lily! Like the pale earnestness of
some lovesick thunder-cloud that longs to grasp
the fleeting lightning in his outstretched arms! He
poured it into the columns of the *Weybridge
Watchman*, the local paper of the town that gave
him birth. Dainty little poems, the dew of his sweet
soul, the tender frothings of his soldier brain. In
them I read him, and in them I loved him! I wrote
to him for his autograph – he sent it. I sent him
my photograph, and directly he saw it he proposed
in terms that cloyed me with the sweet surfeit of
their choice exuberance, imploring me at the same
time to reply by telegraph. Then, maiden-like, I
longed to toy and dally with his love. But Anglo-
Indian telegraphic rates are high; so, much against
my maiden will, I answered in one word - that one
word, yes!

And when will I see him? Alas, never, for (pity
me) he is faithless! We corresponded for a year,
and then his letters ceased; and now, for eighteen
months, no crumb nor crust of comfort has
appeased my parched and thirsting soul!
Fortunately, my solicitor has all his letters. We
have advertised for him right and left. Twenty men
of law are on his track, and my brother Bulstrode,
an attorney's clerk, carries a writ about him night
and day. Thus my heart-springs are laid bare that
every dolt may gibe at them – the whole county
rings with my mishap – its gloomy details are on
every bumpkin's tongue! This – this is my secret.
Swear that you will never reveal it!

Available in *English Plays of the Nineteenth Century, Volume 4.*
Edited by M. R. Booth (Oxford University Press).

THE ANNIVERSARY (1891)

by Anton Chekhov

Anton Pavlovitch Chekhov (1860-1904) needs no introduction as either a playwright or short story writer. Author of the naturalistic masterpieces *The Seagull* (1896), *Uncle Vanya* (1897), *Three Sisters* (1901) and *The Cherry Orchard* (1904) he worked with Stanislavsky at the Moscow Art Theatre. Some of his earlier one-act plays are broadly comic, such as *The Bear* (1888) and *The Wedding* (1889).

The action of The Anniversary *takes places in the offices of the Mutual Credit Bank, on its fifteenth anniversary. Here, the Chairman's young wife arrives from a visit to her family – when her husband was planning an all-male celebration dinner.*

TATYANA (*Out of breath*): Have you missed me? How are you, my darling? I haven't been home yet, I came straight from the station. I've so much to tell you, I couldn't wait. I won't take my coat off, though. I'll be off in a minute. Is all well at home? Good. Mother and Katya send their love. Valisy told me to give you a kiss, so here goes. (*Kisses him.*) Auntie sent a pot of her home-made jam and everyone's furious with you for not writing. Oh yes, Zina sends a kiss too. (*Kisses him again.*) Oh, darling, if you'd any idea what's been going on, if only you knew! What a palava!

But you don't seem very pleased to see me. Oh, of course, it's the anniversary. Congratulations, darling. Congratulations, gentlemen. So today's the meeting and the dinner. Lovely. Remember that lovely address to the shareholders? The one that took you so long to write. Are they presenting that today?

Go home? Yes, of course I'll go home. But I must tell you... I must tell you all about it. From the very beginning. After you saw me off on the train, I sat next to that fat woman, remember? And I started reading. Well, you know how much I hate talking on trains. I read for three whole stops and said not a word, not to anyone. Then it started to get dark and... well, it's always rather depressing when it gets dark, isn't it? There was a young man sitting opposite me, dark hair, quite good-looking – terribly attractive, actually. We fell into conversation. A sailor came along and then some student or other. (*Laughs.*) You'll never guess. I told them I was single and they were all over me. We talked and talked and talked – till long past midnight. The dark young man told screamingly funny stories and the sailor kept singing rather risqué songs! I laughed so much I thought I'd burst. And when the sailor – oh, those sailors! – when he found out I was called Tatyana, he kept singing bits from *Eugene Onegin.*

Sergei met me at the station. Then another young man turned up – a tax inspector, I think he said – and we all got chatting and we all went off for coffee together. The tax inspector had lovely eyes! And the weather! It was glorious.

What? You're busy? Oh dear, have I said the wrong thing? Well, why didn't you say so.

Available in *Chekhov: Short Plays*. Edited by Ronald Hingley (Oxford University Press).

THE MOLLUSC (1907)

by Hubert Henry Davies

Hubert Henry Davies (1869-1917) hailed from Cheshire and was educated at Manchester Grammar School. He worked in the textile industry until 1893 when he went to the USA and produced his earliest plays in New York. Returning to the UK in 1901 he was the author of a number of comedies including *Mrs Gorringe's Necklace* (1903), *Doormats* (1912) and *A Single Man* (1910).

> *MRS BAXTER is a pretty woman of thirty-five, vague in her movements and manner of speaking. Here she is complaining to her husband about her brother's perceived romantic attachment to their governess, MISS ROBERTS.*

MRS BAXTER: I don't like the way Tom is carrying on with Miss Roberts. Last evening they monopolized the conversation. This morning – a walk before breakfast. Just now – as soon as my back is turned – at it again. I don't like it. It wouldn't suit me at all if Tom became interested in Miss Roberts. I could never find another Miss Roberts. She understands my ways so well, I couldn't possibly do without her; not that I'm thinking of myself; I'm thinking only of her good. It's not right for Tom to come here turning her head, and I don't suppose the climate of Colorado would suit her.

That is so like you, dear – to sit and let everything slip past you like the – what was that funny animal Tom mentioned – the mollusc. I prefer to take action. We must speak to Tom. I'll only offend him if I say anything to him. I think it would come much better from you. You know the way men talk to each other. Go up to him and say, 'I say, old fellow, that little governess of ours. Hands off, damn it all.'

MISS ROBERTS enters.

Oh, Miss Roberts. I want a word with you before
you start off on your picnic. Sit down, dear. You
know how devoted I am to my brother Tom. I am
sure you will take what I'm going to say as I mean
it, because – (*Smiles at her.*) I am so fond of you.
Ever since you came to us I have wished to make
you one of the family. When I say, one of the
family, I mean in the sense of taking your meals
with us. Mr Baxter and the girls and I are so much
attached to you. We should like to keep you with
us always. (*Smiling and raising her hand in
protestation.*) Try not to interrupt. I should say that
a man of Tom's age who has never married would
be a confirmed bachelor. He might amuse himself
here and there with a pretty girl, but he would
never think of any woman seriously. To speak quite
frankly – as a sister – I find your attitude towards
my brother Tom a trifle too encouraging. Last
evening, for instance, you monopolized a good
deal of the conversation – and this morning you
took a walk with him before breakfast – and
altogether – (*Very sweetly.*) it looks just a little bit as
if you were trying to flirt – doesn't it?

I didn't say you were a flirt – I said...

We'll say no more about it. It was very hard for me
to have to speak to you. You have no idea how
difficult I found it.

Available in *Late Victorian Plays 1890-1914.* Edited by Geroge
Rowell (Oxford University Press).

THE SCOUNDREL (1868)

by Alexander Ostrovsky

Alexander Ostrovsky (1823-1886) was one of the first major Russian playwrights. His plays include *The Forest* (1871), *The Scoundrel* (1868) and *The Snow Maiden* (1873). Ostrovsky remains very popular in Russia, though his plays have only recently been performed in the West. He writes, above all, about the lives of tradesmen, merchants and minor civil servants and was the first to deal seriously with this introspective, crude and grasping milieu. *The Scoundrel* has also been successfully performed in the West as *Too Clever by Half.*

> *KLEOPATRA ILVOVNA MAMEVA is married to the nouveau-riche MAMAEV and is a great organiser. She tends to sweep everything and everyone before her and her affected manner is both revealing and amusing.*

KLEOPATRA: There's no need for a great brain when you're as handsome as Yegor. What does he want a brain for? He's not going to be a professor. A good-looking young man can always find somebody who'll help him, simply out of sympathy. Either to make a career or just with money so that he can live comfortably. With a clever man it's different. Nobody minds if they see a clever man shabbily dressed, living in a cheap apartment and dining off a cold sausage and a piece of bread – that doesn't bring a lump to your throat and make you feel you must do something for him. You expect a clever man to live like that. But when you see a poor boy who's young and handsome, shabbily dressed, it's unbearable. It mustn't be allowed, no, and it won't be. I'll see that it isn't! The women of Moscow must band together! We must insist that our friends, our husbands, all the authorities rise to their feet to help him. We simply cannot allow a handsome young

man to be spoilt by poverty. There are so few of
them nowadays. Of course, we should sympathise
with all poor people, it's our duty, that goes without
saying – but to see a handsome young man with
sleeves too short, or frayed shirt collars, that's what
touches the heart! And besides, a man can't be bold
and dashing when he's poor, he can't have that
conquering expression, that air of jauntiness which
is so pardonable in a handsome young man.

Available in *Gorky: Five Plays* (Methuen).

THE LADY OF THE CAMELLIAS (1852)

by Alexandre Dumas fils.

The younger Alexandre Dumas (1824-95) was the son of the Alexandre Dumas who wrote such famous novels as *The Count of Monte Cristo* and *The Three Musketeers*. Dumas fils, as he is known, was the successful author of some strong social dramas, including *Le Demi-Monde, Francillon* and *Denise*. The famous *La Dame aux Camellias* began life as a novel and Dumas himself adapted it for the stage. The tragic tale of the consumptive courtesan was an immediate hit and, in turn, became the basis of Verdi's opera *La Traviata*. In modern years, it has often been known as *Camille*, inspiring not only a celebrated 1936 film with Greta Garbo but a more recent re-working of the novel by Pam Gems. What follows, though, is from Dumas' own stage adaptation.

> *MARGUERITE GAUTIER, a celebrated courtesan, lives under the protection of the COMTE DE GIRAY. ARMAND DUVAL, a young man of means, has fallen in love with her and is violently jealous of GIRAY. He declares his love for MARGUERITE, but she believes their love is impossible.*

MARGUERITE: It's better that we don't see each other any more.

There have been moments when I have followed this dream through to the end; there have been days when I have grown sick of the life I'm living now and imagined another life. In the middle of this troubled existence, our minds and our pride and our senses may live but our hearts are suppressed. And when our hearts cannot find a way to express themselves, they suffocate. Women like me are suffocating, Armand. We seem happy. People envy us. But our lovers do not ruin themselves for us, however much they claim to. They ruin themselves for their own vanity. We come first in their self-love, but last in their respect. We have friends, friends

like Prudence, whose affectionate displays are far
from being selfless or disinterested. Why should
they care what we do or what becomes of us as long
as they are seen in our boxes at the theatre or riding
in our carriages in the Bois?

All around us is ruin, shame and lies. I used to
dream of – I've never told anyone this – I used to
dream of meeting a man who was enough of a hero
not to call me to account for what I have done in
the past, who simply wanted to be the lover of my
dreams. The Duke was such a man, but old age is
remarkably unprotective, and remarkably lacking in
comfort. My spirit had needs he could not fulfil.
Then I met you. Look at you! Young, eager, happy.
You shed tears for me, you were concerned about
my health, you even visited me when I was ill...
Your openness, your enthusiasm... these things made
me see in you what I had been crying out for from
the depths of my noisy, lonely life. Like a fool,
without stopping to think, I dreamed a future built
on your love. I dreamed of the countryside, of being
clean again. I remembered my childhood – we were
all innocent once, whatever we may have become –
but it was only a dream, an impossible wish. What
you said to me confirmed that.

You wanted to know what I felt. Now you do.

There are many editions of *The Lady of the Camellias,* and it is
included in the useful anthology, *Mirrors for Man: 26 plays of the
World Drama*. Edited by Leonard Ashley (Winthrop Publishers
Inc, 17 Dunster St, Cambridge, Massachusetts 02138, USA).

THE DEMI-MONDE (1855)

by Alexandre Dumas fils

See note on Dumas on page 42.

In this exposé of Parisian society, the BARONESS SUZANNE D'ANGE visits her former lover, OLIVIER DE JALIN.

SUZANNE: I went to Baden not so much as a woman who wanted to be idle than as one who wanted time to think – like a sensible woman. It's easier to realize what one truly feels and thinks when there is a little distance. Perhaps you were more important to me than I wanted to believe. I went away in order to see whether I could manage without you. I can. You did not follow me; and the most that can be said of your letters is that they were clever. Two weeks after I left, you were completely indifferent to me. When I returned, my first idea was simply to not seek you out but to wait until chance should bring us together. But we are both sensible people, and instead of trying to avoid seeing each other, it is much more dignified to try to have it done with once and for all. So here I am, asking you whether you want to turn our false love into a true friendship? Why do you smile?

Towards the end of my last stay in Paris you did not come to see me as often as you used to. I soon saw that the excuses you gave for not coming – or rather the pretexts you made before not coming – were hiding some mystery. Another woman. What else could it be? The beautiful Charlotte de Lornan? One day when you were leaving my home, saying that you were off to meet some man friend, I followed you. I gave the porter twenty francs, and learned that Madame de Lornan lived

there, and that you went to see her every day. I did
my best to be jealous, and failed. It was that
simple. That's when I understood that I didn't
love you.

If I had spoken to you then about Madame de
Lornan, I should have had to ask you to choose
between us. As she was your more recent conquest,
I should have been sacrificed for her – and my
pride would never have borne that. I didn't want to
speak to you. You are free to love whom you like.
All I ask is your friendship. May I have it? It will
be more difficult than you imagine. I don't mean
by that word 'friendship' one of those banal
commonplaces that every lover offers the other
when they separate; that is nothing more than
mutual indifference. What I want is an intelligent
friendship, a useful attachment, a form of devotion,
protection if need be, and – above all – discretion.
There may be only one occasion, of five minutes
or less, when I shall ask you to prove your
friendship. But that will be enough. Do you accept?

Another translation of this play is available in *World Drama*.
Edited by Barrett H. Clark (Dover Books).

DANTON'S DEATH (1835)

by Georg Büchner

Georg Büchner (1813-1837) had a brief but extraordinary life. He was a biologist, a radical student and was pursued by the authorities for sedition. He died of typhus after producing only three plays, *Danton's Death, Leonce and Lena* (1836) and the fragmentary *Woyzeck* (1837), which was the first working-class tragedy. None of the plays were performed in his lifetime, and his reputation has only grown in the twentieth century, with Alban Berg's opera *Wozzeck*.

> *MARION is a prostitute. She has had an attachment to DANTON, the passionate French Revolutionary leader and here, alone with him, tells him the story of her life.*

MARION: I came of a good family. My mother was an intelligent woman. She brought me up carefully. She always taught me modesty is a great virtue. When people came to the house, if they started to speak of certain subjects she used to send me out of the room; if I asked what they meant she said I ought to be ashamed of myself; if she gave me a book to read, there were almost always some pages I had to leave out. But I could read as much of the Bible as I liked; every page of it was holy. There were some things in it I couldn't understand. I couldn't ask any one; I brooded. Then spring came, and all around me something was happening, something I had no share in. A strange atmosphere surrounded me; it almost stifled me. I looked at my own body; sometimes I felt as if there were two of me, and then again I melted into one. In those days a young man came to visit us; he was handsome and often said silly things to me; I didn't quite know what they meant, but I couldn't help

laughing. My mother made him come often; it
suited us both. In the end we couldn't see why we
shouldn't just as well lie beside each other
between the sheets as sit beside each other on two
chairs. It gave me more pleasure than his
conversation and I didn't see why I should be
allowed the smaller pleasure and denied the
greater. We did it secretly. It went on for some
time. But I was like a sea that swallowed
everything up and sank deeper and deeper into
itself. For me only my opposite existed, all men
melted into one body. It was my nature. Who can
get beyond that? In the end he noticed. One
morning he came and kissed me as if he was
going to suffocate me; his arms closed tightly
round my neck, I was terrified. Then he let me
go, laughed and said he had nearly done a very
stupid thing. He said he didn't want to spoil my
fun too soon, and after all it was the only thing I
had. Then he went away. I still didn't know what
he meant. In the evening I was sitting at the
window. I sank into the waves of the sunset. I am
very sensitive. My only hold on everything
around me is through feeling. A crowd came
down the street, children ran ahead, women
looked out of their windows. I looked down. They
carried him past in a basket. The moon shone on
his pale forehead, his curls were wet – he had
drowned himself. I had to cry. Other people have
Sundays and weekdays, they work for six days and
pray on the seventh, once a year they have a
birthday and feel sentimental, and every year they
look forward to New Year. All that means nothing
to me. For me there are no dates, no changes. I
am always one thing only, an unbroken longing
and desire, a flame, a stream. My mother died of
grief. People point their fingers at me. That is

stupid. Only one thing matters, what people
enjoy, whether it's the body, or holy images, wine,
flowers, or toys; the feeling is the same; those
who enjoy most, pray most.

There is a famous translation by Stephen Spender, originally
published by Faber. Alternatively, there are several editions
of Büchner's *Complete Plays*.

THE CENCI (1819)

by Percy Bysshe Shelley

Percy Bysshe Shelley (1792-1822) is famed as one of the great Romantic poets. He was born in Sussex and educated at Eton and Oxford. His reputation as a radical led to his being sent down from Oxford, and he subsequently travelled widely throughout Europe. His first wife, Harriet Westbrook, was only sixteen when she married him and later drowned herself in the Serpentine. His famous poems include *Ode to a Skylark* (1819) and *Ode to the West Wind* (1819). His two serious attempts at writing plays were this and *Prometheus Unbound*.

Based on the lives of a notorious Roman family, this tragedy deals with the incestuous passion of COUNT FRANCESCO CENCI for his daughter, BEATRICE. Here she talks to her former beloved, ORSINO, who has taken holy orders but who has once again been importuning her with love.

BEATRICE:

Pervert not truth,
Orsino. You remember where we held
That conversation; – nay, we see the spot
Even from this cypress; – two long years are past
Since, on an April midnight, underneath
The moonlight ruins of mount Palatine,
I did confess to you my secret mind.
As I have said, speak to me not of love;
Had you a dispensation I have not;
Nor will I leave this home of misery
Whilst my poor Bernard, and that gentle lady
To whom I owe life, and these virtuous thoughts,
Must suffer what I still have strength to share.
Alas, Orsino! All the love that once
I felt for you, is turned to bitter pain.
Ours was a youthful contract, which you first
Broke, by assuming vows no Pope will loose.
And thus I love you still, but holily,

Even as a sister or a spirit might;
And so I swear a cold fidelity.
And it is well perhaps we shall not marry.
You have a sly, equivocating vein
That suits me not. – Ah, wretched that I am!
Where shall I turn? Even now you look on me
As you were not my friend, and as if you
Discovered that I thought so, with false smiles
Making my true suspicion seem your wrong.
Ah, no! forgive me; sorrow makes me seem
Sterner than else my nature might have been;
I have a weight of melancholy thoughts,
And they forbode – but what can they forbode
Worse than I now endure?
(*Aside.*) Weak and deserted creature that I am,
Here I stand bickering with my only friend!

Available in any complete edition of Shelley's works.

THE STORM (1860)

by Alexander Ostrovsky

See note on Ostrovsky on page 40. *The Storm* became the basis for Janacek's 1921 opera, *Katya Kabanova*.

KATERINA is unhappily married to the violent TIKHON, and their lives are ruled by his tyrannical mother, KABANOVA. KATERINA is in love with BORIS, who lives in fear of his uncle DIKOY. TIKHON escapes his mother's clutches by embarking on a business trip, but refuses to take his wife with him. TIKHON'S unmarried sister, VARVARA, is in love with KUDRYASH and steals a key to enable her and KATERINA to meet KUDRYASH and BORIS. Here, KATERINA is alone in the house, with the key in her hand.

KATERINA: What is she doing? What is she plotting? Oh, she is mad, quite mad! This means ruin! I ought to throw this key away, far away, into the river, where it will never be found! It burns my hands like a live coal. (*After a moment.*) This is how we women are lost. Who wants to live in bondage? All sorts of ideas come into one's head. An opportunity presents itself, and one is glad and makes a headlong plunge. But how can one do that without thinking or considering? It's easy to sin! But once the sin is committed, one spends a whole lifetime weeping; and bondage seems even more bitter.

Pause.

Bondage is bitter, so bitter! Who would not weep? Women, most of all. Take me! I live and suffer and see no escape! And I shan't see any, I know that! The farther I go the worse it will be. And now, to make it worse, I have sinned. If it were not for my mother-in-law! She has ruined me – the house is hateful to me because of her; even the walls are loathsome. (*Looking thoughtfully at the key.*) Shall I throw it away? Of course, I must. Why did it fall into my hands? To tempt me, to ruin me?

She listens.

Someone is coming! (*Hiding the key in her pocket.*) No, there is no one! Why was I so frightened? And I hid the key. Well, that is where it belongs! It is Fate! What sin will it be for me to look at him just once, from a distance? Even if I talk to him, there's really no harm in that! But what did I swear to my husband? But he didn't want me to, himself. Perhaps a chance like this won't come again in my whole life. Then I shall reproach myself: "You had a chance but you weren't clever enough to take advantage of it." What am I saying? Why am I fooling myself? Even if I die, I will see him. Who am I pretending to? Shall I throw away the key! No, not for anything on earth! It is mine now. – Come what may, I shall see Boris! Oh, if only night would come.

Available in *Four Russian Plays*. Translated by Joshua Cooper (Harmondsworth).

CHILDREN OF THE SUN (1905)

by Maxim Gorky

Maxim Gorky (1868-1936) survived a poverty-stricken upbringing and years of wandering to become a national celebrity by the age of thirty. His short stories personified romantic revolt and he became increasingly involved in radical politics as the 1917 Russian revolution approached. His most famous plays are *The Lower Depths* (1902) and *Summerfolk* (1904).

This play depicts the confusions and yearnings of the intelligentsia at the time of the October 1905 revolution. ELYENA is the sister of PAVEL FYODORICH PROTASSOV, a student of Natural Science, and she is talking to VAGUIN, an artist, and her brother.

ELYENA: Dmitri Sergeyich, we all know life is difficult. We get tired of living sometimes, when everything seems so ugly and brutal and there's nowhere to go to rest one's soul. Of course I know beauty is rare, but if you can find it, true beauty lights up the soul like the sun suddenly bursting through the clouds on a dark, grey day... If only everybody could learn to understand and love beauty they'd build a whole ethic around it... they'd judge their actions purely in terms of beauty and ugliness... and then life itself would become beautiful! Art must reflect man's eternal striving towards the distance, towards the heights... when I can sense the presence of this striving in an artist, when I feel he believes in the sunlike power of beauty, then his picture, his book, his sonata will have real meaning for me, will become dear to me... he'll have sounded a harmonious chord in my soul, and if I'm tired I shall feel rested and ready again for life and work and happiness!

You know, sometimes I imagine a painting like this.
A ship comes sailing across a boundless sea. Green,
angry, foaming waves suck greedily at the hull. And
there, up on the prow, I see a group of figures –
strong, powerful men... There they stand, with
smiles on their bold, open faces, gazing ahead... far
ahead into the distance, towards their goal – and
ready to perish calmly, if need be, in the attempt to
get there... That's all there is in the picture! People
like these would walk under a scorching sun across
the desert's yellow sands... These would have to be
really outstanding men, courageous and proud,
unshakeable in their determination... and simple, of
course, as everything great is simple... A picture
like that could make me feel proud of mankind,
proud of the artist who created it... it would remind
me of all the great men who have helped us to move
on, so far from the animals, and who are still
leading us forward towards... full humanity.

Available in *Gorky: Five Plays* (Methuen).

CHILDREN OF THE SUN (1905)

by Maxim Gorky

See note on Gorky on page 53.

*MELANYA is a rich widow, the sister of BORIS
BORISOVITCH CHEPURNOY, a Ukrainian veterinary
surgeon. She is in love with PROTASSOV, who is not
interested in her. She is talking to PROTASSOV's sister,
ELYENA.*

MELANYA (*With a sad smile*): There he goes – it was
nothing, he says, a trifle... I bare my entire soul to
him and he says – it could happen to anyone... as if
I'd stepped on his corn!

Oh, my dear, it's not for me to be offended by him,
is it? I didn't sleep the whole night long, I kept
walking and walking about the house thinking –
how could I have dared to talk to him? And do
you know what it was? – I still had this idea that I
could attract him with money, nobody can resist a
really big sum of money, I thought... But he wasn't
tempted...

You say I should forget it all, but – no, I shan't
forget! I daren't forget, because if I do some
stupidity like that might spill out again. Oh my
dearest, what a horrible old hussy I am! Shameless,
mildewed... I don't have many thoughts, and none
of those I do have are straight – they're like
worms, wriggling in every direction... And I don't
want to have thoughts like that, I don't want them!
I want to be straight and honest... I must be
honest... or else I could do so much harm...

I've been through some hard times. My God, yes,
I've had it hard! I've been kicked and beaten...
shouted at... cursed... but it isn't my ears or my back
I'm sorry for, it's my soul! My soul's been twisted

out of shape, my heart's been dirtied... soiled... It's difficult for me now, to believe in anything good. And what's the point of life, if you can't believe? Boris – well, Boris of course, he just laughs at everything, believes in nothing... And look at him. He's like a stray dog. But you know... when I spoke to you... you believed me straight away! I was amazed! I thought you must be fooling me, but then... you were so gentle and truthful with me... you explained me to myself... and you did it so well, so simply... and it's true, what you said – it isn't me, a female who loves – it's me, a human being... I hadn't felt the human being in me before, I didn't believe in the idea. I understood immediately. But even so, I thought, let's try anyway, I thought, maybe I can buy this funny gentleman, as my next husband. That's how low I am.

Available in *Gorky: Five Plays* (Methuen).

THE SECOND MRS TANQUERAY (1893)

by Sir Arthur Wing Pinero

The Second Mrs Tanqueray is a serious drama, controversial in its day, dealing with the tragic effect of society's rules on a 'woman with a past'. The role made a star of Mrs Patrick Campbell and set a fashion for plays about 'fallen women' (such as Wilde's famous *Woman of No Importance* and *Ideal Husband*). This character can be seen as a direct descendant of Marguerite Gautier in *The Lady of the Camellias*, the courtesan with the pure heart. See note on Pinero on page 15.

Here PAULA, a sophisticated woman with a past, endeavours to set matters straight with her future husband before they marry.

PAULA: Dearest!

Are you angry? I know it's eleven o'clock. I haven't dined, Aubrey dear. In the first place, I forgot to order any dinner, and my cook, who has always loathed me, thought he'd pay me out before he departed. I didn't care. As there was nothing to eat, I sat in my best frock, with my toes on the dining-room fender, and dreamt, oh, such a lovely dinner-party. It was perfect. I saw you at the end of a very long table, opposite me, and we exchanged sly glances now and again over the flowers. We were host and hostess, Aubrey, and had been married about five years. And on each side of us was the nicest set imaginable – you know, dearest, the sort of men and women that can't be imitated. But I haven't told you the best part of my dream. Well, although we had been married only such a few years, I seemed to know by the look on their faces that none of our guests had ever heard anything – anything – anything peculiar about the fascinating hostess. (*With a little grimace.*) I wonder!

(*Glancing at the fire.*) Ugh! do throw another log on.
I've something important to tell you. No, stay where
you are. (*Turning from him, her face averted.*) Look
here, that was my dream, Aubrey; but the fire went
out while I was dozing, and I woke up with a
regular fit of the shivers. And the result of it all was
that I ran upstairs and scribbled you a letter. (*Taking
a letter from her pocket.*) I've given you an account of
myself, furnished you with a list of my adventures
since I – you know. (*Weighing the letter in her hand.*) I
wonder if it would go for a penny. Most of it you're
acquainted with; I've told you a good deal, haven't
I? What I haven't told you I daresay you've heard
from others. But in case they've omitted anything –
the dears – it's all here. It may save discussion by
and by, don't you think? There you are. Take it.
Read it through after I've gone, and then – read it
again, and turn the matter over in your mind finally.
And if, even at the very last moment, you feel you –
oughtn't to go to church with me, send a messenger
to Pont Street, any time before eleven tomorrow,
telling me that you're afraid, and I – I'll take the
blow. It's because I know you're such a dear good
fellow that I want to save you the chance of ever
feeling sorry you married me. I really love you so
much, Aubrey, that to save you that I'd rather you
treated me as – as the others have done. I suppose
I've shocked you. I can't help it if I have.

Available in *Late Victorian Plays 1890-1914.* Edited by George
Rowell (Oxford University Press).

THE SECOND MRS TANQUERAY (1893)

by Sir Arthur Wing Pinero

See note on Pinero on page 15 and on *The Second Mrs Tanqueray* on page 57.

At the end of the play, it becomes clear to PAULA that her marriage to AUBREY TANQUERAY can never work, because of her past. Immediately after this speech she will kill herself.

PAULA (*Matter of fact*): You'll never forget this, you know. Tonight and everything that's led up to it. Our coming here, Ellean, our quarrels – cat and dog! – Mrs Cortleyon, the Orreyeds, this man! What an everlasting nightmare for you.

I believe the future is only the past again, entered through another gate. Tonight proves it. You must see now that, do what we will, go where we will, you'll be continually reminded of – what I was. I see it. You'll do your best – oh, I know that – you're a good fellow. But circumstances will be too strong for you in the end, mark my words. Of course I'm pretty now – I'm pretty still – and a pretty woman, whatever else she may be, is always – well, endurable. But even now I notice that the lines of my face are getting deeper; so are the hollows about my eyes. Yes, my face is covered with little shadows that usen't to be there. Oh, I know I'm 'going off'. I hate paint and dye and those messes, but, by and by, I shall drift the way of the others; I shan't be able to help myself. And then, some day – perhaps very suddenly, under a queer, fantastic light at night or in the glare of the morning – that horrid, irresistible truth that physical repulsion forces on men and women will come to you, and you'll sicken at me. (*Staring forward, as if looking at what she describes.*) You'll see

me then, at last, with other people's eyes; you'll see
me just as your daughter does now, as all
wholesome folks see women like me. And I shall
have no weapon to fight with – not one serviceable
little bit of prettiness left me to defend myself
with! A worn-out creature – broken up, very likely,
some time before I ought to be – my hair bright,
my eyes dull, my body too thin or too stout, my
cheeks raddled and ruddled – a ghost, a wreck, a
caricature, a candle that gutters, call such an end
what you like! Oh, Aubrey, what shall I be able to
say to you then? And this is the future you talk
about! I know it – I know it!

Availabe in *Late Victorian Plays 1890-1914*. Edited by George
Rowell (Oxford University Press).

CAIN (1821)

by George Gordon, Lord Byron

Lord Byron (1788-1824) is primarily known as one of the great Romantic poets, with works including *Childe Harold* (1812), *The Corsair* (1815) and *Heaven and Earth* (1822). In 1816 he left England in self-imposed exile because of what he perceived as the strictures of a hypocritical society. He wrote several verse dramas (containing some fine poetry but negligible as drama) in Pisa in the early 1820s, including *Manfred*, *The Two Foscari* and *Mazeppa*.

The plot concerns the biblical story of CAIN, who in this version becomes a pupil of LUCIFER and subsequently murders his brother ABEL. Here, EVE, the mother of all mankind, has discovered ABEL's death and curses CAIN for all eternity. Other characters on stage are ADAM, CAIN himself and ADAH, ADAM and EVE's daughter.

EVE:

Oh! speak not of it now: the serpent's fangs
Are in my heart. My best beloved, Abel!
Jehovah! this is punishment beyond
A mother's sin, to take *him* from me!
Speak, Cain! and say it was not thou! It was.
I see it now – he hangs his guilty head,
And covers his ferocious eye with hands
Incarnadine.
   Hear, Jehovah!
May the eternal serpent's curse be on him!
For he was fitter for his seed than ours.
May all his days be desolate!
   He hath left thee no brother –
Zillah no husband – me no son! – for thus
I curse him from my sight for evermore!
All bonds I break between us, as he broke
That of his nature, in yon – Oh death! death!
Why didst thou not take me, who first incurr'd thee?

Why dost thou not so now?
(*Pointing to Cain.*) May all the curses
Of life be on him! and his agonies
Drive him forth o'er the wilderness, like us
From Eden, till his children do by him
As he did by his brother! May the swords
And wings of fiery cherubim pursue him
By day and night – snakes spring up in his path –
Earth's fruits be ashes in his mouth – the leaves
On which he lays his head to sleep be strew'd
With scorpions! May his dreams be of his victim!
His waking a continual dread of death!
May the clear rivers turn to blood as he
Stoops down to stain them with his raging lip!
May every element shun or change to him!
May he live in the pangs which others die with!
And death itself wax something worse than death
To him who first acquainted him with man!
Hence, fratricide! henceforth that word is *Cain*,
Through all the coming myriads of mankind,
Who shall abhor thee, though thou wert their sire!
May the grass wither from thy feet! the woods
Deny thee shelter! earth a home! the dust
A grave! the sun his light! and heaven her God!

Available in any complete edition of Byron's poetical works.

THE CORSICAN BROTHERS (1852)

by Dion Boucicault

Dion Boucicault (1820-1890) was an Irish playwright who later became enormously successful in America and became an American citizen. He was a volatile character and had an erratic career, writing a huge number of comedies, dramas and melodramas. Those that have survived into the twentieth century include *London Assurance* (1841), *The Shaughraun* (1880) and *The Colleen Bawn* (1860). *The Corsican Brothers* is based on a novel by Alexandre Dumas père and was notable for having one actor play both of the eponymous brothers.

Here EMILIE DE LESPARRE, a pure young woman of character, meets her former betrothed, CHÂTEAU-RENAUD, in the lobby of the Paris Opéra.

EMILIE: You requested my presence here; I am come, although at the risk of my motives being misinterpreted by you and by the world. I have obeyed the conditions you demanded; now keep your promise and restore to me those letters. Give them to me at once, and let me go.

My first affections, as you know, were yours; my father saw and crushed our hopes at once. The fate of my poor sister, the miserable marriage of Louise, was ever present to his mind. A marriage which lost him a daughter – me a sister. Unhappy girl, where is she now? Perhaps deserted, struggling with misery and want. Some cause, of which I am ignorant, taught his distempered mind to see in you a copy of my sister's husband. To snatch me from the fate he so much dreaded, he obliged me to accept the hand of the Admiral de L'Esparre. The disparity of our years, our total want of sympathy, rendered it impossible for me to love, although I respect and honour him. It is now a sacred duty I owe to my husband, as well as myself, to claim from you the evidences of our plighted troth. Be not deluded by a thought so vain, so false, as to suppose I can again receive you with the feelings that inspired those letters: cease to claim possession of a heart which, with all its sufferings, all its anguish, belongs now to another; such sentiments are unworthy of you, and their avowal tends to degrade us both. Those letters have been seen by others, and thus through the thoughtlessness of vanity, you assist to wound the honour you are bound to guard. I cannot disregard the warning of a friend. The letters – I implore you – the letters ...

There are several editions of this, and it is included in *Collected Plays of Dion Boucicault* (Cambridge University Press).

THE FATHER (1887)

by August Strindberg

August Strindberg (1849-1912) is, with Ibsen and Chekhov, one of the founding fathers of modern drama. He explored the psyche, particularly in relation to sexuality, as well as pioneering non-naturalistic forms of drama in such works as *Dream Play* (1907), *The Ghost Sonata* (1908) and the *To Damascus* trilogy (1900). He wrote more than sixty plays between 1870 and his death, including *The Dance of Death* (1905), *Miss Julie* (1888) and *The Stronger* (1890), all of which contain good speeches for women.

> *The Father is one of Strindberg's naturalistic dramas, dealing with a battle fought at a psychological level between LAURA and her husband, the CAPTAIN, for their daughter BERTHE. This scene comes at the beginning of the play, shortly after we have met LAURA and her eccentric husband. She is talking to DOCTOR OSTERMARK, who is new to the area. Here, she is attempting to recruit him to her side for the battle that will follow.*

LAURA: Welcome, Doctor! I am delighted to see you! The Captain is out, but he'll be back in a few minutes. Do sit down, won't you? There's a lot of illness about at present. I hope you'll get on all right. In a lonely country district like this it's wonderful to find a doctor who takes an interest in his patients. I have heard so many nice things about you, Doctor, that I hope we shall be on the best of terms. We have been lucky enough to escape acute illnesses; still, things are not quite what they should be. I'm sorry to say not all what we might wish them to be! There are things in a family which one's conscience and sense of honour compel one to conceal from the world... (*Taking out her handkerchief.*) My husband is not quite right in his mind. He has the most extraordinary ideas sometimes. As a scientific man, of course, he has a

right to them – as long as they don't have a
disturbing influence on the welfare of his family.
For instance, he has an absolute craze for buying
everything he possibly can! Whole cases full of
books, which he never reads. Don't you believe
me? Is it reasonable to say that one can see in a
microscope what is happening on another planet?
That's what he says. Yes, in a microscope. You
don't believe me, Doctor. Here I am, telling you
all about our family secret, and... He shows
symptoms of a capricious mood, a vacillation of
will. We have been married twenty years, and he
has never yet come to any decision without
changing his mind afterwards! He is obstinate, too.
He always insists on getting his own way; but the
moment he has got it, he drops the whole thing
and begs me to decide for him. God knows how I
have taught myself to meet his wishes through all
these long years of trial! Oh, if you only knew
what a life of struggle I have gone through at his
side! If you only knew!

There are several versions of Strindberg's plays in various
translations, including a major series published by Jonathan
Cape. Perhaps the most accessible are *Strindberg Plays: One,
Two and Three* (Methuen).

THE TYRANNY OF TEARS (1899)

by Charles Haddon Chambers

Charles Haddon Chambers (1860-1921) was an Australian of Irish parentage who arrived in England in 1880 and had his first play performed by 1886. He was a successful commercial playwright, writing for such contemporary stars as Irene Vanbrugh and Sir Gerald du Maurier. His plays include *The Idler* (1890), *The Fatal Card* (1894), *Passers-by* (1911) and *The Saving Grace* (1917).

> *In this middle-classes comedy, set in PARBURY's study, MR PARBURY is unable to work because of his wife's interference, and announces that he is going away for a few days accompanied by his secretary, MISS WOODWARD. MRS PARBURY, 'a pretty, fragile little woman of about twenty-eight' misunderstands the situation and demands MISS WOODWARD's resignation.*

MRS PARBURY: It is quite impossible for Miss Woodward to stay. Miss Woodward leaves this house in the morning. (*With assumed brightness.*) Now, darling, it will be different. Of course, I couldn't say much before her. You were quite right to be nice and courteous to her now she is going. Oh, she *is* going, believe me she is. Of course, we don't want to be hard on her, and she shall have a month's salary and a strong recommendation. You must leave this matter to me. There are some things that men can't be trusted to know about.

She takes his arm and talks rapidly, gradually rather hysterically, towards the end appearing about to cry.

Darling, do listen. You don't understand. You have never been like this with me before. I'm sure I'm not asking very much. You can easily get another secretary. Another time you shall have a man one, as you originally wanted to. You were right, dear – you often are. Darling, do be reasonable. I've been a good wife to you, haven't I? I've always respected your wishes, and not bothered you more than I could help. This is only a little thing, and you must let me have my own way. You must trust me absolutely, dear. You know anything I would do would only be for your good, for you know that I love you. (*She takes out her handkerchief.*) I adore you, darling. You must give way – you must – you must!

I wasn't going to cry. I had no intention of crying, dear. Shall I write out an advertisement for you, dear? For a new secretary – a man.

Clement!

Oh, I understand now. You use this exaggerated language, you make these cruel accusations, you work yourself into a passion, because you have grown to think more of Miss Woodward than of me. What? Me, cry? (*Puts handkerchief up her sleeve, controls her anger, and becomes very determined.*) You are quite wrong. Probably I shall never again know the relief of tears. Your callousness and obstinacy seem to have dried up all the tenderness in me. Miss Woodward leaves this house in the morning, or I leave it tonight.

Available in *English Plays of the Nineteenth Century, Volume 3.* Edited by M. R. Booth (Oxford University Press).

LA SAINTE COURTISANE

by Oscar Wilde

Oscar Fingal O'Flahertie Wills Wilde (1854-1904) is one of the most famous figures in late nineteenth century drama, the flamboyant and ultimately disgraced author of such plays as *Salomé* (1892), *Lady Windermere's Fan* (1892), *An Ideal Husband* (1895) and *The Importance of Being Earnest* (1895) as well as the ground-breaking novel *The Picture of Dorian Gray* (1891). *La Sainte Courtisane* is a fragment of an early work and the style is reminiscent of *Salomé*.

> *MYRRHINA is a lubricious courtesan who will, during the course of the drama, be converted to Christianity by a Roman soldier, HONORIUS. Here she talks of her erotic triumphs.*

MYRRHINA: My chamber is ceiled with cedar and odorous with myrrh. The pillars of my bed are of cedar and the hangings are of purple. My bed is strewn with purple and the steps are of silver. The hangings are sewn with silver pomegranates and the steps that are of silver are strewn with saffron and with myrrh. My lovers hang garlands round the pillars of my house. At night time they come with the flute players and the players of the harp. They woo me with apples and on the pavement of my courtyard they write my name in wine.

From the uttermost parts of the world my lovers come to me. The kings of the earth come to me and bring me presents.

When the Emperor of Byzantium heard of me he left his porphyry chamber and set sail in his galleys. His slaves bare no torches that none might know of his coming. When the King of Cyprus heard of me he sent me ambassadors. The two Kings of Libya who are brothers brought me gifts of amber.

I took the minion of Caesar from Caesar and made him my playfellow. He came to me at night in a litter. He was pale as a narcissus, and his body was like honey.

The son of the Praefect slew himself in my honour, and the Tetrarch of Cilicia scourged himself for my pleasure before my slaves.

The King of Hierapolis who is a priest and a robber set carpets for me to walk on.

Sometimes I sit in the circus and the gladiators fight beneath me. Once a Thracian who was my lover was caught in the net. I gave the signal for him to die and the whole theatre applauded. Sometimes I pass through the gymnasium and watch the young men wrestling or in the race. Their bodies are bright with oil and their brows are wreathed with willow sprays and with myrtle. They stamp their feet on the sand when they wrestle and when they run the sand follows them like a little cloud. He at whom I smile leaves his companions and follows me to my home. At other times I go down to the harbour and watch the merchants unloading their vessels. Those that come from Tyre have cloaks of silk and earrings of emerald. Those that come from Massilia have cloaks of fine wool and earrings of brass. When they see me coming they stand on the prows of their ships and call to me, but I do not answer them. I go to the little taverns where the sailors lie all day long drinking black wine and playing with dice and I sit down with them.

I made the Prince my slave, and his slave who was a Tyrian I made my Lord for the space of a moon.

I put a figured ring on his finger and brought him to my house. I have wonderful things in my house.

The dust of the desert lies on your hair and your feet are scratched with thorns and your body is scorched by the sun. Come with me, Honorius, and I will clothe you in a tunic of silk. I will smear your body with myrrh and pour spikenard on your hair. I will clothe you in hyacinth and put honey in your mouth.

Available in *Complete Works of Oscar Wilde* (Collins).

THE LOWER DEPTHS (1902)

by Maxim Gorky

See note on Gorky on page 53. *The Lower Depths* is considered his masterpiece. It is a story of low-life surviors, living in a Moscow doss house.

> *NASTYA is a prostitute, alcoholic and fantasist, who insists on regaling her companions with invented tales of her former life.*

NASTYA: And so, at dead of night, into the garden he came, to the summer-house, as had been arranged between us. I had long been awaiting him there, trembling with fear and grief. He too was trembling all over and as white as a sheet, and there ... in his hands ... a revolverer! And in a fearful voice he says to me, 'Ah, my precious love, my pearl without price! My sweetest love,' he says. 'My parents,' he says, 'will not give their consent to our marriage, and,' he says, 'they say they will curse me for all eternity because of my love for you. On which account,' he says, 'I am obliged to take my life.' And he had this revolverer, an enormous great thing it was and loaded with ten bullets. 'Farewell!' he says, 'gentle friend of my heart! I have taken an irreversable decision, for I cannot possibly live without you.' And I answered him, 'Oh, my never to be forgotten friend, Raoul...'

What do you mean, 'Last time it was Gaston!' Shut up... you... you mangy dogs! How could you ever understand love – true love? And that's what mine was – *true!* (*To the Baron.*) You – you're nothing! Supposed to be an educated man, supposed to have drunk coffee in bed with cream in it...

Shan't tell any more. Don't want to. If they're not going to believe me, if they're going to laugh at me ...

Suddenly breaking off, NASTYA is quiet for a few seconds and then, closing her eyes again, she starts to talk passionately and loudly, her hand beating time to her words, as if she is listening to music in the distance.

And so I answered him, 'Oh light of my life! heart of my heart! No more could I possibly live in this world without you, for I love you quite insanely, and ever will I love you while my heart beats within my breast! But,' says I, 'do not, oh do not take your own young life, for your dear parents so badly need you to live, you who are their only joy! No, no, rather leave me, forget me, rather let me perish with grief over the loss of you who are my whole life... I am alone in the world... let me be... forsaken... doesn't matter... I'm no good... nothing... I'm nothing... there's nothing here for me... nothing...

Available in *Gorky: Five Plays* (Methuen).

DEIRDRE (1907)

by W. B. Yeats

William Butler Yeats (1865-1939) was one of the leading lights of the Irish theatrical renaissance of the 1890s and early 1900s. He was dedicated to the formation of an Irish National Theatre and, with Lady Gregory, established the pre-eminence of Dublin's Abbey Theatre. He was a distinguished poet as well as playwright, and many of his verse plays are based on Irish myths. His most famous plays include *The Countess Cathleen* (1892), *On Baile's Strand* (1904), *Cathleen ni Houlihan* (1902) and the *Cuchulain* cycle, celebrating the great Celtic warrior and mystic.

> *DEIRDRE tells the old Irish folk tale of Deirdre of the Sorrows. DEIRDRE was the daughter FEDLIMID, harper to KING CONCHUBAR of Ulster. CATHBAD the Druid foretold that her beauty would bring banishment and death to heroes. COCHUBAR had destined her for his wife and had her brought up in solitude, but she fell in love with NAOISE, son of USNACH, who carried her off to Scotland. CONCHUBAR lured them back and treacherously slew NAOISE. Here, DEIRDRE pleads with CONCHUBAR for the chance to lay out NAOISE's corpse. She will subsequently kill herself.*

DEIRDRE:

O, do not touch me. Let me go to him.

Pause.

King Conchubar is right. My husband's dead.
A single woman is of no account,
Lacking array of servants, linen cupboards,
The bacon hanging – and King Conchubar's house
All ready, too – I'll to King Conchubar's house.
It is but wisdom to do willingly
What has to be.
You thought that I would curse you and cry out,
And fall upon the ground and tear my hair.

(*Laughing.*) You know too much of women to think so;
Though, if I were less worthy of desire,
I would pretend as much; but, being myself,
It is enough that you were master here.
Although we are so delicately made,
There's something brutal in us, and we are won
By those who can shed blood. It was some woman
That taught you how to woo: but do not touch me:
I shall do all you bid me, but not yet,
Because I have to do what's customary.
We lay the dead out, folding up the hands,
Closing the eyes, and stretching out the feet,
And push a pillow underneath the head,
Till all's in order; and all this I'll do
For Naoise[1], son of Usna.
(*Motioning Conchubar away.*) No, no. Not yet. I cannot
        be your queen
Till the past's finished, and its debts are paid.
When a man dies, and there are debts unpaid,
He wanders by the debtor's bed and cries,
'There's so much owing.'
You'll stir me to more passion than he could,
And yet, if you are wise, you'll grant me this:
That I go look upon him that was once
So strong and comely and held his head so high
That women envied me. For I will see him
All blood-bedabbled and his beauty gone.
It's better, when you're beside me in your strength
That the mind's eye should call up the soiled body,
And not the shape I loved. Look at him, women.
He heard me pleading to be given up,
Although my lover was still living, and yet
He doubts my purpose. I will have you tell him
How changeable all women are; how soon
Even the best of lovers is forgot
When his day's finished.
(*Almost with a caress.*) It is so small a gift and you
        will grant it

[1] Pronounced 'Neesha'

Because it is the first that I have asked.
He has refused. There is no sap in him;
Nothing but empty veins. I thought as much.
He has refused me the first thing I have asked –
Me, me, his wife. I understand him now;
I know the sort of life I'll have with him;
But he must drag me to his house by force.
If he refuses (*She laughs.*), he shall be mocked of all.

Available in *W. B. Yeats: Collected Plays* (Macmillan).

THE DUCHESS OF PADUA

by Oscar Wilde

See note about Oscar Wilde on page 69. *The Duchess of Padua* is a very early play, not professionally performed in Wilde's lifetime – and rarely since. It is a full-blown romantic verse melodrama in which Beatrice, the Duchess, sacrifices everything for her adulterous love of young Guido Ferranti.

In a dungeon in the public prison of Padua, GUIDO lies asleep, condemned for the murder of the DUKE OF PADUA. Determined to save her beloved, the DUCHESS arrives masked and gains entry to the cell.

THE DUCHESS:

(*Taking her mask off.*) At last!
He can escape now in this cloak and vizard,
We are of a height almost: they will not know him;
As for myself what matter?
So that he does not curse me as he goes,
I care but little: I wonder will he curse me,
He has the right. It is eleven now.
They will not come till twelve. What will they say
When they find the bird has flown?

Goes over to the table.

So this is poison.
Is it not strange that in this liquor here
There lies the key to all philosophies?

Takes up the cup.

It smells of poppies. I remember well
That, when I was a child in Sicily,
I took the scarlet poppies from the corn,
And made a little wreath, and my grave uncle,
Don John of Naples, laughed: I did not know
That they had power to stay the springs of life,

To make the pulse cease beating, and to chill
The blood in its own vessels, till men come
And with a hook hale the poor body out,
And throw it in a ditch: the body, ay, –
What of the soul? that goes to heaven or hell.
Where will mine go?

Takes the torch from the wall, and goes over to the bed.

        How peacefully here he sleeps,
Like a young schoolboy tired out with play:
I would that I could sleep so peacefully,
But I have dreams.

Bending over him.

      Poor boy: what if I kissed him?
No, no, my lips would burn him like a fire.
He has had enough of Love. Still that white neck
Will 'scape the headsman: I have seen to that:
He will get hence from Padua to-night,
And that is well. You are very wise, Lord Justices.
And yet you are not half so wise as I am,
And that is well.
      O God! how I have loved you,
And what a bloody flower did Love bear!
What if I drank these juices, and so ceased?
Were it not better than to wait till Death
Come to my bed with all his serving men,
Remorse, disease, old age, and misery?
I wonder does one suffer much: I think
That I am very young to die like this,
But so it must be. Why, why should I die?
He will escape tonight, and so his blood
Will not be on my head. No, I must die;
I have been guilty, therefore I must die.
He loves me not, and therefore I must die.
I would die happier if he would kiss me,
But he will not do that. I did not know him.
I thought he meant to sell me to the judge;

That is not strange; we women never know
Our lovers till they leave us.

Bell begins to toll.

Thou vile bell,
That like a bloodhound from thy brazen throat
Call'st for this man's life, cease! thou shalt not get it.
He stirs – I must be quick.

Takes up cup.

O Love, Love, Love,
I did not think that I would pledge thee thus!

Drinks the poison.

Available in *Complete Works of Oscar Wilde* (Collins).

ENEMIES (1908)

by Maxim Gorky

See note on Gorky on page 53. *Enemies* was one of Gorky's most controversial works, being based closely on recent political events and was banned by the authorities.

TATIANA, an actress now married to YAKOV BARDIN, talks of her despair.

TATIANA: This place is oppressive. Everything's crumbling, it makes my head spin in the strangest way. One has to tell lies, and I don't like doing that. But I've just told a lie – I said I'd talk to Nadya about hiding something – she'd have agreed, too. But I've no right to start her on that road. Those people do sometimes take liberties. It's all so strange. Not long ago life was so clear and simple, one could see what one wanted. I did once think that on the stage my feet were planted in solid ground... that I might grow tall...
(*Emphatically, with distress.*) But now it's all so painful – I feel uncomfortable up there in front of those people, with their cold eyes saying, 'Oh, we know all that, it's old, it's boring!' I feel weak and defenceless in front of them, I can't capture them, I can't excite them... I long to tremble in front of them with fear, with joy, to speak words full of fire and passion and anger, words that cut like knives, that burn like torches... I want to throw armfuls of words, throw them bounteously, abundantly, terrifyingly... so that people are set alight by them and shout aloud, and turn to flee from them... And then I'll stop them. Toss them different words. Words beautiful as flowers. Words full of hope and joy, and love. And they'll all be weeping, and I'll weep too... wonderful tears. They applaud. Smother

me with flowers. Bear me up on their shoulders.
For a moment – I hold sway over them all... Life is
there, in that one moment, all of life, in a single
moment. Everything that's best is always in a
single moment.

How I long for people to be different – more
responsive, less careful – and for life to be
different, not all hustle and bustle, a life in which
art is needed, always, by everybody, all the time!
So I could stop feeling ... totally superfluous...

Available in *Gorky: Five Plays* (Methuen).

RIDERS TO THE SEA (1904)

by J. M. Synge

John Millington Synge (1871-1909) was educated at Trinity College, Dublin and subsequently travelled to Paris where, in 1899, he met W. B. Yeats. Yeats persuaded Synge to apply his talents to describing Irish peasant life, and Synge went on to be one of the leaders of the 'Irish Renaissance' in the early years of the twentieth century. He is the author of a number of remarkable plays including *The Playboy of the Western World* (1907), *The Shadow of the Glen* (1903), and *The Well of the Saints* (1905).

> Riders to the Sea *is a short folk-tragedy, set on an island off the west of Ireland. MAURYA is an old peasant woman, vanquished by natural forces – the death of a son by drowning – and she accepts her fate with remarkable stoicism and dignity.*

MAURYA: (*In a low voice, but clearly.*) It's little the like of him knows of the sea... Bartley will be lost now, and let you call in Eamon and make me a good coffin out of the white boards, for I won't live after them. I've had a husband, and a husband's father, and six sons in this house – six fine men, though it was a hard birth I had with every one of them and they coming to the world – and some of them were not found, but they're gone now, the lot of them... There were Stephen, and Shawn, were lost in the great wind, and found after in the Bay of Gregory of the Golden Mouth, and carried up the two of them on the one plank, and in by that door.

There was Sheamus and his father, and his own father again, were lost in a dark night, and not a stick or sign was seen of them when the sun went up. There was Patch after was drowned out of a curagh[1] that turned over. I was sitting here with

---

[1] small sailing craft, like a coracle or canoe

Bartley, and he a baby, lying on my two knees, and I seen two women, and three women, and four women coming in, and they crossing themselves, and not saying a word. I looked out then, and there were men coming in after them, and they were holding a thing in the half of a red sail, and water dripping out of it – it was a dry day, Nora – and leaving a track to the door.

There does be a power of young men floating round in the sea, and what way would they know if it was Michael they had, or another man like him, for when a man is nine days in the sea, and the wind blowing, it's hard set his own mother would be to say what man was it.

They're all gone now, and there isn't anything more the sea can do to me... I'll have no call now to be up crying and praying when the wind breaks from the south, and you can hear the surf is in the east, and the surf is in the west, making a great stir with the two noises, and they hitting one on the other. I'll have no call now to be going down and getting Holy Water in the dark nights after Samhain[2], and I won't care what way the sea is when the other women will be keening.

There are several editions of this play, and it is included in *Selected Plays and Poems of J. M. Synge* (Everyman).

---

[2]The equivalent of Allhallows Eve, falling on November 1st and marking the beginning of winter. It is celebrated with harvest rites and a Feast of the Dead.

Also published by Oberon Books in association
with LAMDA:

Solo Speeches for Men (1800-1914)
ISBN: 1 84002 046 6

Solo Speeches for Women (1800-1914)
ISBN: 1 84002 003 2

Contemporary Speeches for Young Women
ISBN: 1 84002 130 6

The LAMDA Anthology of Verse and Prose, Vol XV
ISBN: 1 84002 120 9

The Lamda Guide to English Literature
ISBN: 1 84002 011 3

Classics for Teenagers
ISBN: 1 84002 023 7

Solo Scenes for Under 12s
ISBN: 1 84002 013 X

Meaning, Form and Performance
ISBN: 1 870259 74 2

First Folio Speeches for Men
ISBN: 1 84002 015 6

First Folio Speeches for Women
ISBN: 1 84002 014 8